ADVANCE PRAISE FOR *JEANNETTE RANKIN,
BRIGHT STAR IN THE BIG SKY*

"*Bright Star* is a clear portrayal of one of America's most
significant women and of the times in which she lived.
This book is a splendid tool for teaching the younger
generation about Jeannette Rankin's work for peace,
suffrage, and the rights of women and children."

Lynn Tennefoss, Director
Jeannette Rankin Peace Resource Center
Missoula, Montana

ISBN 1-56044-360-X

50795>

9 781560 443605

Bright Star
in the Big Sky

FALCON™

Jeannette Rankin
—— *1880–1973* ——

Bright Star
in the *Big Sky*

by Mary Barmeyer O'Brien

A Two Dot Book

© 1995 by Falcon Press Publishing Co., Inc.,
Helena and Billings, Montana.

Cover photo: UPI/Bettmann
Title page photo (pg. 5): Montana Historical Society, Helena

Design, typesetting, and other prepress work by Falcon Press, Helena, Montana.

Library of Congress Cataloging-in-Publication Data
O'Brien, Mary Barmeyer.
        Jeannette Rankin : 1880-1973 : bright star in the big sky / by
    Mary Barmeyer O'Brien.
            p.   cm.
        Includes bibliographical references.
        ISBN 1-56044-265-4. -- ISBN 1-56044-360-X (pbk.)
        1. Rankin, Jeannette--Juvenile literature. 2. Legislators--United
    States--Biography--Juvenile literature. 3. United States.
    Congress. House--Biography--Juvenile literature.   I. Title.
    E748.R223O28   1995
    328.73'092--dc20
        [B]   95-8656
                                                                      CIP

Printed in U.S.A.

For my parents, Dorothy D. and George H. Barmeyer, who have always been my bright stars in the Big Sky.

Acknowledgments

Special thanks to Virginia Ronhovde, Jeannette Rankin's niece; Don Spritzer, reference librarian at Missoula Public Library; and Pat Ortmeyer of Missoula's Jeannette Rankin Peace Resource Center who each read my manuscript for precision of detail prior to its publication.

I am also indebted to Polson City Librarian Marilyn Trosper and to Dave Walter, research historian with the Montana Historical Society, for their assistance with my research, and to Bette Ammon and Don Spritzer of Missoula Public Library for their written support of this project. I'd like to express my gratitude to fellow writers Maggie Plummer and Woodeene Koenig-Bricker for their valuable advice, to the schoolchildren who read the manuscript and offered me their fresh perspectives, and especially to my family and friends who were a constant source of encouragement and support.

Contents

One: A LONE VOTE 13

Two: MONTANA GIRLHOOD 19

Three: SOCIAL WORK AND SUFFRAGE 27

Four: FIRST WOMAN IN CONGRESS 35

Five: STANDING BY HER COUNTRY 43

Six: PEACE WORKER IN GEORGIA 49

Seven: A WOMAN'S JOB 55

Eight: DOING ALL WE CAN FOR PEACE 63

BIBLIOGRAPHY 69

---- *One* ----

A LONE VOTE

Silence fell over the U.S. Congress. A crowd of restless lawmakers and visitors quieted as they waited for Representative Jeannette Rankin to speak. The moment had come for the congresswoman from Montana to cast her vote.

It was December 8, 1941. Up to that day, the United States of America had been able to stay out of the dreadful conflict called World War II. But tragedy had struck a few hours before. Japanese warplanes had bombed Pearl Harbor, the U.S. Navy's largest base in the Pacific Ocean. More than 3,500 people had been killed or wounded during the surprise attack. Huge ships had sunk into the once-peaceful Hawaiian harbor. The bombing raid had destroyed U.S. Army and Navy planes by the hundreds.

Shock, anger, and grief rocked the nation.

Almost immediately, President Franklin D. Roosevelt responded to the country's outrage. He asked Congress to declare war on Japan.

Most people hoped every lawmaker would vote "yes" so that the Japanese would be sent a forceful, unanimous message. They believed the attack on a U.S. naval base had made the situation clear, and that the time had come for their country to join the side of the Allies in the conflicts then raging around the globe.

But sixty-year-old congresswoman Jeannette Rankin of Montana believed war was wrong. For the previous twenty years she had worked night and day to bring about world peace. She had voted against war once before in Congress. In everything she did, Jeannette struggled to end war forever.

She also had a promise to keep. When she campaigned for Congress, she had told Montanans that if she was elected she would help keep their sons out of World War II.

She had tried to explain her views. "Mr. Speaker!" she had called out as Congress discussed President Roosevelt's request for a declaration against Japan. "I would like to be heard!" Again and again she tried to speak against the war. Again and again, despite her bold efforts, she was ignored or shouted down by the Speaker of the House and other congressmen. "Mr. Speaker!" she exclaimed.

But the clerk had begun reading the roll call. As their names were read, the representatives voted aloud. Each one had said "yes" to declaring war on Japan. Jeannette Rankin was next on the list.

As the clerk called her name, Jeannette looked up and squared her shoulders. In her clear, strong voice, she spoke the words that would change her life forever. "No," she said.

"As a woman I can't go to war, and I refuse to send anyone else."

Instantly an outcry rose from the crowd. Spectators hurled protests and insults at the woman who had voted for peace. Hissing and booing filled the chambers.

The voting went on until every member of the House of Representatives had given his or her opinion. The Senate also voted. All together, 470 lawmakers said "yes" to war.

Only Jeannette Rankin voted "no."

As the crowd began to leave, Jeannette gathered her things and stepped into the coatroom. Visitors weren't allowed there, but they pressed around her anyway, angry about her proud, lone vote.

Some accounts of that moment say Jeannette was pushed and grabbed by the furious mob. Concerned but unafraid, she looked for a way to escape. When she spotted a nearby telephone booth, she slipped inside and shut the doors behind her. Then she dialed the Capitol switchboard and asked for the building's police.

The officers arrived promptly. Before long, they broke up the crowd and escorted Jeannette to her office. All day they stood guard outside.

The nation's anger toward the one peaceful representative continued for weeks. For her stand against the war, Jeannette was called "stupid," "ignorant," and a "disgrace to Montana." Cruel and angry letters flooded in, ordering her to resign and go back to her home state. Some demanded that she change her vote immediately. Others warned that

UPI/BETTMANN

Troubled by angry crowds just after her lone vote against the nation's entry into World War II, Jeannette slipped into a telephone booth where she dialed Capitol police for help. This photo appeared in newspapers across the country the next day.

she would never be re-elected. Even her brother told her gruffly, "Montana is 110 percent against you."

Still, a few people praised her enormous courage.

Although public comment ran against her, Jeannette received letters of support from across the nation. Author Lillian Smith wrote, "That one little vote of yours stands out like a bright star in a dark night." And although nearly all Montana newspapers found fault with Jeannette, the *People's Voice* from Helena praised her "splendid example of courage and conviction . . . "

Later in life, she was asked if she had ever regretted her vote. "Never," she replied with complete certainty. "If you're against war, you're against war regardless of what happens. It's a wrong method of trying to settle a dispute." She said that she would vote against war today, tomorrow, and forever.

In the days after the vote, however, when her office phones jangled angrily or the mail carrier brought another stack of unpleasant letters, Jeannette would sometimes close her eyes for just a moment. Perhaps she thought about the green meadows of the western Montana ranch where she played as a girl. She might have remembered her comfortable childhood home in the nearby town of Missoula where she and her siblings grew up. Maybe she pictured these early years to remind herself of a more peaceful time and place.

Two

MONTANA GIRLHOOD

Twelve-year-old Jeannette Rankin perched on the back of her parents' jolting hay wagon. The cool Montana air that blew across her face smelled of ponderosa pine. Occasionally a meadowlark flew up from the new grass, or a white-tailed deer darted into the thickets along the road. Up front, Jeannette's parents, John and Olive Rankin, talked amid the chattering voices of their children.

At last summer had come! Jeannette was glad to see the gravel streets of Missoula disappear behind them as her father guided the creaking wagon through rutted tracks toward their ranch house ahead. Winter in town had seemed endless that year.

All winter, Jeannette had gone to school in Missoula. Although she enjoyed classroom challenges and learned quickly, her blue eyes often wandered from the teacher. She looked out the window and daydreamed about the world beyond. Memorizing ordinary facts didn't interest her.

Jeannette learned more from listening to the intelligent conversations between her parents and their friends. They often had long fireside talks about government, history, and faraway places. Sometimes they told the story of Chief Joseph, the courageous and peace-loving leader of the Nez Perce Indians. Later in her life, Jeannette would remember his example of quiet bravery when his fleeing band was pursued and finally stopped by U.S. soldiers. "I will fight no more forever," he had said, preferring peace to war.

Who could guess that these conversations would follow Jeannette her whole life? Who would have thought that the ideas growing within her would someday make her one of the best-known women in the nation?

Her family's winter discussions held her interest, but Jeannette favored the busy summers on the Rankin ranch, six miles from town. She had been born in the ranch house on June 11, 1880, nine years before Montana Territory became a state. Her father was then a young Scottish-Canadian carpenter, and her mother was a schoolteacher who had come west from New England. Eventually Jeannette would have five younger sisters and a brother: Philena (who died in childhood), Harriet, Wellington (the only boy), Mary, Grace, and Edna.

The hay wagon came to a stop at the ranch house door. Jeannette pushed back her brown hair, jumped down, and began to help her mother and father unload the summer supplies. As she worked, she kept a careful watch over her younger sisters playing in the tall grasses.

Montana was still a frontier state in 1892, and life was

Portrait of the Rankin family about 1895. Back row, left to right: John, Jeannette, Harriet, Wellington, and Olive. Seated in front, left to right: Mary, Edna, and Grace. Philena, who died in childhood, is picutured in the photograph on the table.

sometimes hard then. On the West's many farms and ranches, men and women had to labor side by side as equals to survive. They shared much of the rough outdoor work and the never-ending daily chores. But in many other ways men and women were not equal, and young Jeannette noticed this. For instance, whenever an election came up, women were not allowed to vote. Women had no say about the laws that affected them. Elected officials on even a local level were almost always men.

Jeannette thought about this as she cleaned, sewed, and cared for the younger children on the ranch that summer.

She sometimes grew impatient with housework and slipped away to ride horseback, exploring the ranch's far corners. Once in a while, she even crept off to peek at the noisy sawmill on the property, although she had been told to stay away from it.

Jeannette sometimes surprised the folks around her. One day her father was lifting hay into a barn with a new piece of equipment when the machine lurched to a halt. The hired hands tried without success to find the problem. Jeannette, who had been watching on the side, quickly pointed out where the machine was stuck. Soon it was running again.

Another time, one of the ranch hands rode up on a horse that had a gaping cut on its shoulder. Jeannette knew the wound had to be treated immediately. She asked the ranch hand to wrestle the horse to the ground while she ran for a needle, thread, and hot water. With her small, strong hands she cleaned and sewed up the gash.

She reacted just as calmly when a ranch dog caught its foot in a trap. Although she tried to force them, the trap's steel jaws could not be opened. Jeannette's quick judgment told her that in order to save the dog she had to amputate its foot. Carefully she did, and afterwards made a little leather boot to protect the stump of its leg. Some say the dog wore this boot until the end of its life.

Jeannette was like her father in many ways. They both had an easy, cordial way with others and were independent thinkers. Over the years, they shared ideas as they worked together on the ranch. John Rankin had no doubt that his daughter Jeannette would accomplish important things in her lifetime. But in at least one way, Jeannette and her father were different. John Rankin was sometimes known to settle arguments with other men using his fists: Jeannette believed strongly in using only words. She believed conflicts could be settled without violence.

The summer of 1892 passed quickly. On the Rankin ranch, the hay and grain turned a deep gold. Soon the fragrant apples in the orchard ripened, and the family began the hot work of canning. Along with the ranch chores they found time, too, for picking sweet serviceberries, entertaining friends and relatives, and dancing to fiddle music at barn gatherings.

J.L. ALLISON/MONTANA HISTORICAL SOCIETY, HELENA

The beautiful Rankin home in Missoula, Montana. Built in 1884, the house stood until the 1950s when it was torn down to make room for a new bridge across the Clark Fork River.

But all too soon, the harvest season ended. It was time for Jeannette and her family to move back to town.

A builder during winter months, John Rankin had constructed a large house in Missoula for his family. He and many others claimed it was the finest home in town. It had a long porch, hot and cold running water, a modern heating system, and the city's first metal bathtub.

In their Missoula home, as on the ranch, Jeannette was a great help to her mother and father. As she grew older, she took on more and more of the household jobs, especially helping to raise her three youngest sisters.

Jeannette also continued to surprise people with her energy and know-how. On one occasion, she even built a sidewalk. When her father said that he was having trouble renting a building he owned because it had no wooden sidewalk in front, Jeannette went to work. She had watched her father's carpentry and knew what to do. With tools and nails, she laid the planks and finished the job. Her father was able to rent the building because of her work.

During her high school years, Jeannette grew into a slender, pretty woman with a good sense of humor. She had dark hair, which she wore pulled back from her face. She laughed from her straight, friendly mouth and had an honest, intelligent look in her eyes. In her spare hours, she read, went ice skating on the Clark Fork River, played basketball (until she broke her nose in the middle of a game), and spent time with her many friends. She and her younger brother Wellington formed a special friendship that lasted throughout their lives.

MONTANA HISTORICAL SOCIETY, HELENA

Jeannette and other young women playing basketball. Jeannette is the third player from the left.

John and Olive Rankin believed strongly in education. They dreamed that each of their children would go to college, even though it was somewhat unusual for women to do so at that time. After graduating from high school in 1898, Jeannette did as her parents had dreamed. She entered the brand-new Montana State University in Missoula.

As she began her college courses and the next phase of her life, she wondered what lay ahead.

MONTANA HISTORICAL SOCIETY, HELENA

Jeannette studied hard, but not always eagerly, at Montana State University in Missoula, where she wrote her senior essay on snail shells. She is shown here in a science lab.

Three

SOCIAL WORK AND SUFFRAGE

"Go! go! go!" Jeannette Rankin told herself in her diary. "It makes no difference where, just so you go! go! go!" But for Jeannette, it did make a difference. She spent the next twelve years traveling, studying, and searching for her life's work.

Jeannette worked hard at Montana State University. After earning a degree in biology and finishing college in 1902, she was undecided about what to do next. For a while she taught school. Then, restless and still living at her parents' home, Jeannette tried dressmaking and furniture design. She considered, but decided against, several marriage proposals. She even took a train east to visit her brother Wellington, who was studying at Harvard University at the time.

It was in Boston, Massachusetts, that Jeannette first saw big-city slums. The desperate living and working conditions on the East Coast disturbed her. She saw children as young as six years old working long, hard days in dirty factories. Many people labored in unsafe conditions, and others had no jobs at all. Families lived in terrible poverty and misery. Even after she returned to Missoula, Jeannette found that the things she had seen in Boston bothered her. She wanted to do something to improve conditions for the poor, but did not know the best way to help.

Jeannette felt as if her life had no direction. In addition to her personal turmoil, she felt a family loss. Her father died of Rocky Mountain Spotted Fever. Jeannette grieved for him intensely.

She decided to try something new. At the age of twenty-eight, she moved to San Francisco, California, where she spent her time helping poor people in the city better their lives. Certain that she had found her calling, Jeannette decided she needed more schooling to prepare for a career in social work. She enrolled in the New York School of Philanthropy. In the nation's largest city, she worked in the poorest slums as part of her studies. Jeannette liked this work of helping others much better than the dressmaking or teaching she had tried in Montana.

Jeannette tried out her new humanitarian skills in other places, too—back in her home town of Missoula, and in the state of Washington. While briefly attending the University of Washington in Seattle in 1910, she made a discovery that sparked something inside of her. The people of Washington were preparing to vote on woman suffrage—that is, the right of women to vote.

Jeannette was excited by this possibility. She remembered her sense of injustice that most women did not have the right to help make laws. She felt if women could vote, they would pass laws that were more gentle and sensitive to the needs of the people. She began traveling up and down the sidewalks of Seattle for the cause, pasting up posters and organizing suffrage meetings.

Even when she was asked to work for suffrage in Ballard, Washington, a community near Seattle that was against women voting, nothing stopped her. Fellow suffragists later told her, "After we saw what you could do in Ballard, we knew we could use you!"

At last, after months of hard work, the suffrage amendment passed in Washington state. Women could vote there! Only four other states had passed such laws. As Jeannette rejoiced at their success, she began to think about her home state of Montana. Could she help a suffrage amendment pass there, too?

While she was home in Missoula for Christmas that year, she had a courageous idea. She sent word to the Montana legislature that she would like to speak to the lawmakers about voting rights for women. She signed her name as a member of the "Equal Franchise Society," a group she had helped organize in the small capital of Helena.

Jeannette was given permission to speak. It wouldn't be an easy job. For eight years the all-male Montana legislature had been discussing suffrage, often joking and laughing about it. Jeannette had to convince them the issue of women's votes was serious and important.

The chambers in the state capitol were crowded on February 1, 1911, the day of Jeannette's speech. She was well prepared. She had practiced her talk many times in front of

MONTANA HISTORICAL SOCIETY, HELENA

Jeannette holding a banner in support of suffrage.

her brother Wellington. Facing the powerful audience, Jeannette lifted her chin and started to speak. As the lawmakers listened, they began to see that suffrage was no laughing matter.

Less than four years later — on November 3, 1914 — Montana women gained the right to vote.

Jeannette had led the way for women's voting rights in Montana. She had learned new ways to organize and campaign in the process. And she had made a name for herself. Men and women alike knew this brave and successful young Montanan and respected her voice in politics.

Jeannette's next political idea excited her even more. In the history of the United States, no woman had ever been elected to the U.S. Congress in Washington, D.C. Jeannette decided she would run for a congressional seat, hoping that she would be the next representative from the state of Montana.

MONTANA HISTORICAL SOCIETY, HELENA

Thirty-year-old Jeannette when she addressed members of the Montana legislature in 1911 and urged them to pass a suffrage amendment. It was the first time Jeannette had spoken before such an imposing crowd, and the first time a woman had ever given a speech to the Montana legislature.

MONTANA HISTORICAL SOCIETY, HELENA

Jeannette and brother Wellington in front of the Rankin home in Missoula, Montana.

— Four —

FIRST WOMAN IN CONGRESS

Some of Jeannette's friends responded to her idea with disbelief. "Congress?" they asked. Could she be serious about running for such a high office? It was a job only men had held before.

But Jeannette was not discouraged. With Wellington as her campaign manager, she began to urge voters to support her. Other candidates for Congress, all men and seven of them Republicans like Jeannette, campaigned too. But the young woman kept going, traveling across Montana and working to win the election. Week after exhausting week she drove from place to place on rugged dirt roads. Storms, mud holes, and flat tires slowed her progress. Still she pushed on.

Montana was huge, Jeannette realized. In the eastern part of the state, thousands of square miles of golden, windswept plains stretched as far as she could see. Remote ranches dotted the landscape. Up and down the state's western section ran the rugged Rocky Mountains, their highest peaks forming

Jeannette's campaign photograph, which helped Montana voters learn to recognize her name and face.

the Continental Divide, the nation's backbone. Blue-gray peaks glistening with snowfields jutted up from cool mountain valleys. The state included more than 147,000 square miles.

Because of the vast terrain and the poor roads, Jeannette sometimes traveled by train. Cramped in a swaying passenger car behind a sooty locomotive, she planned ways to reach every voter in the state. At each stop, she gave at least one speech and listened to the concerns of the Montanans she met.

Sometimes Jeannette stood on a street corner and asked one or two people who were passing by to stop and listen. Then she began to talk about things that mattered to her. It was so unusual to see a young woman speaking to the public on the street that crowds often gathered. Jeannette would then tell her listeners about her support for woman suffrage and the well-being of children. She explained her desire to keep the United States out of World War I, which had started in Europe by then.

She spread her ideas to people in many Montana towns. In the copper-mining city of Butte, she spoke to tired, dusty miners about safer working conditions. In other places she talked with lumberjacks, ranchers, or railroad workers. Saloon customers gathered on the streets to listen to her. Women and children heard her speak at potluck suppers, county fairs, and one-room schoolhouses. Jeannette's mother and sisters had left their homes to campaign for Jeannette, too. As the election grew closer, Jeannette's followers tacked up her posters on trees and sent out hundreds of penny postcards to urge voters to choose Rankin for Congress.

By November 1916, Jeannette had covered thousands of miles. She had visited Montana's larger towns and its remote ranches and homesteads. She had worked tirelessly toward election day and her goal. Finally, the day for voting arrived.

As a Montana woman, Jeannette was able to vote for the first time that year. As she cast her ballot for herself, she wondered if her fellow Montanans would elect her to Congress. She knew it would be a great thing for the nation since, in most states, women were still denied the right to vote.

That evening, Jeannette was bitterly disappointed. The daily newspaper in Missoula said that she was lagging behind in the election and that she had almost certainly lost. Tired and discouraged, she went to bed.

Over the next few days, however, the news changed. As more and more ballots were counted by hand, it became clear that Jeannette Rankin was catching up to her opponents. By the end of the week she had won the election—by more than 7,500 votes.

Jeannette had done it! She had become the first woman elected to the U.S. Congress. Her victory echoed nationwide, and even further. Historians believe she was the first woman in the world ever elected to a national governing body.

All over the United States, newspapers reported the event. Headlines read WOMAN TO BE IN CONGRESS and RANKIN'S ELECTION IS NOW SURE. Reporters and photographers surrounded Jeannette's home. Letters poured in. As far away as France, people wanted to know more about the progressive young woman from Montana. "To suddenly be thrown into such publicity," Jeannette later recalled, "was a great shock. It was very hard for me to comprehend—to realize that it made a difference what I did do and didn't do from then on." She said that she felt an enormous responsibility to all Montanans and to women everywhere.

When the time came, Jeannette was prepared for her first day in national government. On April 2, 1917, a parade of cars took her through the streets of Washington, D.C., to the nation's Capitol. As she entered the chamber of the House of Representatives, her fellow elected officials who were gathered there stood up and cheered. They clapped warmly as she was escorted to her place.

Jeannette stayed calm and poised throughout the day. She smiled and shook hands cordially, and bowed with dignity to the applause. Spectators could see immediately that the carefully dressed thirty-six-year-old Montanan was intelligent and refined.

Still smiling, the first congresswoman took her place amid the rows of men.

Just before Jeannette was driven to the nation's Capitol on April 2, 1917 to be introduced as the first congresswoman, she gave a speech from the balcony of the National American Woman Suffrage Association headquarters. Beside her is Carrie Chapman Catt, another foremost suffragist.

MONTANA HISTORICAL SOCIETY, HELENA

Jeannette Rankin carrying a bouquet of flowers on her first day in Congress.

Five

STANDING BY HER COUNTRY

"**M**iss Rankin?"

On her sixth day as a congresswoman, Jeannette did not answer when she heard her name called. She was being asked to cast her first vote in Congress. The clerk of the House was waiting for her answer. But who could have expected that she would have to make such an agonizing decision so soon?

Cameras, congressmen, and friends in the balcony stared as she struggled to decide how she should cast her vote. Should she say yes to entering World War I—against her deepest beliefs—or disappoint her suffragist friends, her brother Wellington, and thousands of Montana voters by saying "no" as her heart demanded? Deeply troubled, she remained silent. She would delay voting until the roll call was read a second time.

During the short wait, pictures swirled through Jeannette's mind.

She remembered Wellington walking with her to the

Capitol, saying a "no" vote would alienate her voters and end her new career.

She recalled a disturbed President Woodrow Wilson asking Congress to support the war motion against Germany "to make the world safe for democracy."

She imagined suffragists crowding into her office, insisting a "no" vote would show the world women were weak and couldn't face the hardships of war and politics. A "yes" vote, they said, would show women's strength and patriotism.

She thought of the misery, grief, and despair that war brought. She pictured the many men already dead in Europe and thought about their shortened lives.

She remembered the children she had seen in the Boston slums and thought of all the others who needed Congress to pass new laws that might improve their lives.

She pictured masses of women waiting for legislation that would give them the right to vote, while lawmakers focused their attention only on war and wartime needs.

"Miss Rankin?" the clerk asked again.

Jeannette rose to her feet. She took a deep breath and let her words be heard across the otherwise silent chambers. "I want to stand by my country," she said, "but I cannot vote for war. I vote no."

Reports say forty-nine other lawmakers joined her in saying "no," but Jeannette Rankin was singled out for criticism. Newspapers falsely said she cried or fainted while voting. Suffragists felt she had betrayed them. Many Montanans thought her decision came from weakness and that she was unpatriotic.

MONTANA HISTORICAL SOCIETY, HELENA

Representative Rankin working in her office. She completed much of her congressional business here, and with the help of her office staff (which included her sister Harriet), she answered the stacks of mail that arrived each day.

But Jeannette knew she had done the right thing. "I'd go through much worse treatment," she said later. "If you know a certain thing is right, you can't change it."

Still, most members of Congress had voted to declare war. So to Jeannette's dismay, the United States entered World War I. Eighteen months of bitter fighting followed, and many U.S. soldiers were killed.

But Jeannette had come to Washington, D.C., to focus on other things. Despite the uproar over the war, she spent the next two years working for her beliefs and for the needs of the poor. She also supported the suffragists' cause. On

MONTANA HISTORICAL SOCIETY, HELENA

Jeannette (holding the shovel) planting a Montana fir tree on the lawn of the U.S. Capitol. Behind her is the Capitol dome, which is said to have been encircled by doves, a symbol of peace, just before Jeannette voted against U.S. entry into World War I.

January 18, 1918, Jeannette opened congressional debate on a resolution that called for a suffrage amendment. If passed, the proposed change in the U.S. Constitution would grant all women in the nation the right to vote.

The resolution passed the House of Representatives, with Jeannette casting a strong "yes" vote. Unfortunately, the proposed amendment was then defeated in the Senate. The next year, however, a similar resolution won in both chambers. With approval from the states, it became the Nineteenth Amendment to the Constitution of the United States, guaranteeing all women of legal age the right to vote.

"If I am remembered for no other act," Jeannette said, "I want to be remembered as the only woman who ever voted to give women the right to vote." But she is remembered for other things, too. During her term in Congress, Jeannette also worked on a bill to encourage better health for mothers and their infants. And since she hadn't forgotten the young children she had seen working in Boston factories, she pushed for laws to end child labor.

As her two years of being a representative ended, Jeannette wondered if she should run for re-election. Believing in the work she had done, she decided to run for Congress again, this time for a seat in the Senate. Once more she began a long and tiring campaign across Montana.

But Jeannette's "no" vote against World War I had stuck in the minds of Montana voters. Many were still angry about it. In spite of another active campaign, she lost the election this time. Regretfully, she prepared to leave Washington, D.C.

Six

PEACE WORKER IN GEORGIA

As Jeannette left her congressional office in 1919, she had a clear goal in mind. She intended to continue her work for peace and for the welfare of women and children everywhere.

She started in on her plan immediately. Boarding a huge ship, she sailed across the Atlantic Ocean to Europe, where she joined other women from all over the world for a peace conference. They formed the well-known Women's International League for Peace and Freedom.

After she returned to the United States, Jeannette knew she had to find a place to live where she could work toward her goals. She spent the next few years searching for a location where people would be open-minded to her ideas. She also wanted to be close to Washington, D.C., and New York City. And she wanted to be able to live simply. Finally she chose the perfect spot: Georgia.

In Georgia, Jeannette found an old sixty-four-acre

homestead. It had a plain one-room cabin, and no running water or electricity. She bought it for five hundred dollars. Many friends traveled there to see her. In order to have room for them, Jeannette added several small rooms to the cabin. Even then, she continued to use candles or lanterns for light. She installed an old car radiator and used it as a homemade heater. A bucket served as her sink, and a large funnel connected to a hose drained water into the yard. In her rustic kitchen, painted tarpaper covered the walls.

Children from surrounding homesteads often gathered at Jeannette's cabin. On warm summer evenings, they clustered

Jeannette standing beside her plain country home near Athens, Georgia, which she liked to consider a "center of infection" from which a peace epidemic could spread.

Known for her public speaking skills, Jeannette is shown giving one of her many speeches.

around her as she told them stories about Montana, her term in Congress, and her ideas for world peace. She also organized social clubs for the children. Together they read, cooked, or played games. Some learned to sew bathing suits, while others worked on building crystal radios. Sometimes they sliced and ate sweet watermelons. Perhaps they even tasted Jeannette's famous lemon meringue pie.

But most of Jeannette's time was spent working for peace. She became part of several action groups and even organized one herself—the Georgia Peace Society. As the years passed, she worked long hours and traveled thousands of miles giving

A/P WIDE WORLD PHOTOS

In 1932, Jeannette led a motorcade tour from Washington, D.C. to Chicago to urge political parties to include peace plans in their platforms.

talks about peace. She tried to get new laws passed that would make war illegal. As she had done before, she wrote letters supporting nonviolent ways of settling disputes. She set up peace booths at county fairs and urged others to take action toward making the world a better place. When elections came up, she campaigned for peace candidates.

Jeannette was saddened that her efforts did not eliminate war. In fact, as the 1930s progressed she could see signs that another terrible war would soon break out in Europe.

When a fire burned her homestead to its foundation in 1935, Jeannette bought a simple seventy-five-year-old house near Watkinsville, Georgia. Surrounded by tall, green oaks, her modest home became known as "Shady Grove." She covered the earthen floor in one room with imported rugs and moved in.

During her years in the South, Jeannette often visited faraway Montana. Staying with her brother Wellington on his big ranch there, she heard all the news of what was happening in her home state. Her family members were well known in the region. Wellington had become a wealthy and prominent Montana lawyer. Jeannette's sister Edna is believed to have been the first female attorney who had been born in the state. She was known for her work helping women plan the number of children they had. Harriet and Mary became educators, and Grace chose a career in homemaking. Jeannette had many nieces and nephews.

But Jeannette was the most famous of the Rankin siblings. By the late 1930s, she was known throughout the nation as a strong leader of the country's pacifists (people who believe in peaceful solutions to the world's problems). She had spoken many times before Congress, advocating peace. She had broadcast talks on radio, urging national leaders and U.S. citizens to avoid war. As World War II began overseas, she urged her country to stay out of it. "Preparation for war leads to war," she had warned in 1934. "If we are to have peace, we must achieve peace by preparing for it."

Jeannette had perfected her public speaking style. She had a clear voice that carried well and she seemed to speak personally to each member of the audience. She had the ability to make war seem pointless. "You can no more win a war than you can win an earthquake," she once commented.

"If there was a Jeannette Rankin in every state," one person remarked, "our country would never go to war."

Still, World War II spread like a fever. More and more countries entered its ferocious battles. As the 1940s approached, many people thought the United States should join, too.

Jeannette was then nearly sixty years old, and her wavy hair was white. For the previous twenty years, she had devoted her life to peace. Her strong feelings about war had not changed. Each day she became more distressed as she watched her country move closer to entering another global conflict. Carefully, she studied the situation. What more could she do to preserve the nation's peace?

The answer was clear. She must return to Montana and run again for Congress.

—•◦•— *Seven* —•◦•—

A WOMAN'S JOB

Once again, Jeannette crisscrossed Montana campaigning for Congress. And once again, Montanans listened to what she said. A few voters were still angry about her vote against World War I twenty-three years earlier, but most of them admired her work for peace and liked her promise to help keep U.S. soldiers out of World War II.

In November 1940, Jeannette was once again elected to the House of Representatives. Thanks in part to her earlier work for suffrage, she was no longer the only congresswoman. Other women had followed her lead and were now familiar faces on Capitol Hill. For the next several months, Jeannette tried to stop the United States from entering World War II. Several times she brought peace bills before lawmakers, but each time they were voted down.

Then came Japan's sudden attack on Pearl Harbor and President Franklin Roosevelt's request for declaration of war. This time, Jeannette knew in an instant what her vote must

1940 campaign photograph of Jeannette at age 60. One of her friends, New York mayor Fiorello La Guardia, said of Jeannette at the time: "This woman has more courage and packs a harder punch than a regiment of regular-line politicians."

be. She also knew that her decision would be extremely unpopular.

The morning after the Pearl Harbor attack, December 8, 1941, Jeannette drove alone around the streets of Washington, D.C. She didn't want to speak to the many people who would try to persuade her to say "yes" to the inevitable vote on war. Later that day, Jeannette cast her famous lone "no" vote. At that moment, she became the only lawmaker to have voted against both world wars.

After she had escaped the angry mobs outside the telephone booth, Jeannette sat at her desk and wrote a letter to Montanans explaining her action. Her words were printed in several newspapers across the state. "When I cast the only vote against war, I remembered the promises I had made during my campaign for election to do everything possible to keep this country out of war. . ." she said. She repeated that she had voted according to her convictions.

Once again, during her term in office, Congress bustled to make war arrangements. Jeannette wanted no part of this. Instead, she worked briskly to prevent huge profits from being made from the war business. She even suggested payments to help families whose men were overseas. A year later, Jeannette wrote a statement for the Congressional Record. In it, she suggested that President Roosevelt had possibly expected Japan's attack on Pearl Harbor. She felt an investigation was needed. Since that time, others have agreed with her.

While in Congress the second time, Jeannette also spent long hours convincing women that they must work for peace.

MONTANA HISTORICAL SOCIETY, HELENA

Jeannette riding horseback at her brother Wellington's Avalanche Ranch in Montana.

"Peace is a woman's job," she said over and over again. She followed her own advice.

When her second term was over, Jeannette did not run for re-election. She knew she had very little chance of winning after her never-to-be-forgotten vote against World War II. Instead she returned to Montana where her mother, Olive Rankin, was ninety years old and needed care. Jeannette stayed by her side for the next few years. Once home, she helped Wellington run for the U.S. Senate, although his bid was unsuccessful even with her expert campaign help.

In 1946, Jeannette left her mother in the capable hands of nurses while she traveled to India. She wanted to study other nations and learn their ideas for world peace.

"Why India?" her friends asked.

Jeannette replied that she had learned about a great leader there: Mohandas K. Gandhi. Gandhi was a remarkable man who was making huge changes in India's government using peaceful methods. Jeannette admired him very much and wanted to learn from him. She found that Gandhi was very busy with his work when she arrived there, so she decided to wait until her next trip to meet him.

She returned home to Montana, and was there when her mother died in 1947. Jeannette, her brother, and her sisters said good-bye to the pioneer woman who had helped raise their exceptional family.

Over the next twenty years, Jeannette made six more trips to India. She was never able to meet Gandhi, however, because the peaceful protester was assassinated in 1948. Jeannette was deeply disappointed at his death and her lost chance. Even so, she continued to study his ideas.

Jeannette enjoyed India more than many other places. With the hot sun beating down upon her old Ford, which she had shipped from home, she once crossed the entire country. Sometimes she stayed among native people as she learned more about Gandhi's ways of bringing about peace. Other times she stayed at a comfortable hotel in Bombay, overlooking the shining Arabian Sea. During the hot season she occasionally went north to the mountains, the high, cool Himalayas that may have reminded her of her Montana home.

Jeannette's travels covered a large part of the world. This photo shows Jeannette visiting Asia.

She met with officials and attended peace meetings. Everywhere, she was greeted with friendly respect.

India was not the only country Jeannette visited. During the same twenty years she also traveled to places in South America, Africa, Asia, and Europe. Whether she went alone or with a friend, she was never an idle tourist. In each place, Jeannette studied the ways people lived, and she spread her ideas about world peace.

Between trips, Jeannette spent her time at her house in Georgia or on Wellington's busy ranch. Wellington had become one of the wealthiest landowners in Montana, and

MONTANA HISTORICAL SOCIETY, HELENA

Through her seventies and eighties, Jeannette continued to explore the world. In this picture she visits Giza, Egypt.

he helped pay for her trips abroad. He liked to be part of the new ideas Jeannette was gathering. He also ran once more for public office in Montana but again was not elected.

As she grew older, Jeannette was bothered by a painful medical condition called tic douloureux, which affected the nerves in her face. She tried not to let it interrupt her life. At one point she had an operation to try to correct it, but the surgery was only partly successful. Jeannette continued to explore the world in spite of her health, and traveled throughout her seventies and into her eighties. As she visited many countries, her beliefs about peace were made stronger than ever.

In the 1960s, the United States became involved in yet another war overseas. Jeannette watched as troops were sent to the conflict in Vietnam. Although she had purposely stayed out of the public spotlight for more than twenty years, she knew she couldn't sit quietly on the sidelines while this latest war in the jungle raged on.

―――― ❧ ――――

— *Eight* —

DOING ALL WE CAN
FOR PEACE

On January 15, 1968, an event took place that put Jeannette's name back in the news. The Jeannette Rankin Peace Brigade, an impressive march for peace, moved through the streets of Washington, D.C. Named in her honor, the march was Jeannette's way of opposing the war in Vietnam, where ten thousand soldiers had already died.

Jeannette's idea was to protest the fighting with a peaceful parade of ten thousand women. The participants would march to the Capitol and present their requests to lawmakers there. With her usual energy and self-confidence, she helped plan the gigantic gathering.

On the day of the brigade, women began arriving in the cold, wet weather at dawn. Within a few hours, several thousand people from all over the country had assembled. Young and old, rich and poor, dark-skinned and light, they began to march side by side. Mothers carried babies or pushed strollers. Older children walked. People in wheelchairs rolled along with the crowd.

The parade of protesters stretched for several blocks. Many women carried signs for peace. Most were dressed in black. All were strongly against the Vietnam War. And at the head of them all, with her head held high, marched Jeannette Rankin. She was eighty-eight years old.

UPI/BETTMANN

The Jeannette Rankin Peace Brigade marching for peace in Washington, D.C. on January 15, 1968. Jeannette (wearing glasses) is in the center holding the banner.

When at last they reached the Capitol, Jeannette and a small group of leaders stepped forward. They went up the huge stone steps carrying a peace petition, a written request to end the war. This they gave to House Speaker John McCormack and Senate Majority Leader Mike Mansfield, another famous Montana statesman. They had given a strong message against fighting by using nonviolence.

The Jeannette Rankin Peace Brigade didn't end the conflict in Vietnam. But it helped call national attention to the fact that many people were against the war. In the months after the march, Jeannette made public speeches opposing the war. She appeared on national television and was the subject of articles and books. She also was chosen as the first member of the Susan B. Anthony Hall of Fame, a memorial that honors people who have helped promote women's rights in outstanding ways. She received many other awards for her lifetime of work.

Despite her great age, Jeannette had a young mind. She read, studied, and tried new ideas. She had many children and students as friends and loved to listen to their opinions even as physical difficulties slowed her.

Three months before she turned ninety years old, Jeannette fell on the steps of a drugstore and broke her hip. Although she hoped to be able to walk again by her birthday, she was still in a wheelchair when the day arrived. But at her birthday celebration in Washington, D.C., her many notable guests saw that the small ninety-year-old stateswoman was the same strong, independent leader they had always known. They gave speeches praising Jeannette as a trailblazer and held her up as a fine example of rare courage. She was never afraid, they said, to stand up for what she thought was right.

Jeannette continued to voice her ideas and even considered running for Congress again. She was only stopped as, gradually, her health began to fail. Leaving her home in Georgia, she moved to an apartment in Carmel, California, where she would be near her sister Edna.

There, Jeannette Rankin died in her sleep on May 18, 1973. She was almost ninety-three years old.

Twelve years after Jeannette's death, a statue of her was placed in the U.S. Capitol. She and the western artist Charles M. Russell were the only two Montanans to have received such an honor. The bronze statue of Jeannette was sculpted by Mary Theresa Mimnaugh, an artist from Great Falls, Montana. When it was presented to the public, many well-known people spoke about Jeannette's life. She was praised as a "forward thinker," a "remarkable woman," and a "proud Montanan." They admired her honesty and charm. She was hailed as one of the greatest women the country had ever known.

Those who knew her best remembered Jeannette's own words when she once said: "Wouldn't it be too bad if we left this world and hadn't done all we could for peace?"

She herself had no reason for regret. As a symbol of her lifelong work, Jeannette's famous words, "I cannot vote for war," are carved in the statue's base. Today, people from all nations follow her example and work for a world with-out war.

DARRIN A. SCHREDER

This statue of Jeannette Rankin, by sculptor Mary Theresa Mimnaugh, stands in Montana's capitol. It is an exact replica of the Jeannette Rankin statue in the U.S. Capitol.

Bibliography

BOOKS

Acceptance and Dedication of the Statue of Jeannette Rankin 1880-1973. Washington, D.C.: U.S. Government Printing Office, 1987.

Block, Judy Rachel. *First Woman in Congress: Jeannette Rankin.* New York: Contemporary Perspectives, Inc., 1978.

Cohen, Stan. *Missoula Country Images, Vol. II.* Missoula, Montana: Pictorial Histories Publishing Co. Inc., 1993.

Giles, Kevin S. *Flight of the Dove: The Story of Jeannette Rankin.* Beaverton, Ore.: The Lochsa Experience, Touchstone Press, 1980.

Josephson, Hannah. *First Lady in Congress: Jeannette Rankin.* Indianapolis and New York: The Bobbs-Merrill Co., Inc., 1974.

Lang, William L., and Rex C. Meyers. *Montana, Our Land and People.* Boulder, Colo.: Pruett Publishing Co., 1979.

Malone, Michael P., and Richard B. Roeder. *Montana: A History of Two Centuries.* Seattle and London: University of Washington Press, 1977.

Millis, Walter. *Road to War: America 1914-1917.* Cambridge, Mass.: Riverside Press, 1935.

White, Florence Meiman. *First Woman in Congress: Jeannette Rankin.* New York: Julian Messner, 1980.

UNPUBLISHED MANUSCRIPTS/SPEECH TEXTS

Schaffer, Ronald. "Jeannette Rankin, Progressive Isolationist." Ann Arbor, Mich.: University Microfilms, 1970.

Wilson, Joan Hoff. "The Search For Jeannette Rankin's Past." Text of address to the Montana Library Association, Bozeman, Montana. May 4, 1979.

PERIODICALS

Board, John C. "Jeannette Rankin: The Lady From Montana," *Montana: The Magazine of Western History* 17 (July 1967): 2-17.

Brown, Mackey. "Montana's First Woman Politician— A Recollection of Jeannette Rankin Campaigning," *Montana Business Quarterly* (Autumn 1971): 23-26.

Kennedy, John F. "A Woman of Courage," *McCall's* (July 1958): 43-44.

McNamee, Wally. "The Women March," *The Washington Post,* January 16, 1968.

Rankin, Jeannette (ghostwritten by Katharine Anthony). "What We Women Should Do," *Ladies' Home Journal* (August 1917): 17.

Harris, Ted C. "Jeannette Rankin in Georgia," *The Georgia Historical Quarterly* (Spring 1974): 55-78.

Larson, T. A. "Montana Women and the Battle for Ballot: Woman Suffrage in the Treasure State," *Montana: The Magazine of Western History* (winter 1973): 34.

Rankin, Jeannette. Excerpt from statement to *The Missoulian,* December 10, 1941.

Walter, Dave. "Rebel With a Cause," *Montana Magazine* (November/December 1991): 66-72.

Wilson, Joan Hoff. "Jeannette Rankin and American Foreign Policy: The Origins of Her Pacificism," *Montana: The Magazine of Western History* (winter 1980): 28-41.

Wilson, Joan Hoff. "Jeannette Rankin and American Foreign Policy: Her Lifework as a Pacifist," *Montana: The Magazine of Western History* (spring 1980): 38-53.

Winestine, Belle Fligelman. "Mother Was Shocked," *Montana: The Magazine of Western History* (summer 1974): 70-79.

REFERENCE

Constitution of the United States, Nineteenth Amendment.

Congressional Record. "Woman Suffrage Speech of Hon. Jeannette Rankin of Montana in the House of Representatives," January 10, 1918.

Encyclopedia Americana, International Edition. New York: Americana Corporation, 1977.

United States Federal Census for 1900, Missoula County, Hellgate Township, ED 67, Sheet 3, Lines 44ff.

World Book Encyclopedia, vols, 1-18. Chicago: Field Enterprises, Inc., 1953.

VIDEO

"The Woman Who Voted No," produced by Ronn Bayly, Nancy Landgren, and Susan Regele. UM Materials Service, 29 minutes.

Sound Recordings

"Interview with Jeannette Rankin," by John Board, Missoula, Montana. August 29, 1963.

"Interview with Winfield Page," (regarding Jeannette and Wellington Rankin), by Helen Ward Bonner, July 9, 1980.

"Interview with Vivian Halinan," (regarding Jeannette Rankin) by Helen Ward Bonner, July 16, 1980.

"Interview with Belle Winestine," by Helen Ward Bonner.

"Interview with Tom Haines" (former assemblyman and acquaintance of Jeannette Rankin), by Helen Ward Bonner, Missoula, Montana. July 8, 1980.

About the Author

Mary Barmeyer O'Brien was born and raised in Missoula, Montana, and received a B.A. from Linfield College in McMinnville, Oregon. Her magazine articles for both children and adults have appeared in many national publications including *NorthwestLiving!*, *Ladies' Home Journal*, *Jack and Jill*, *Catholic Parent*, *Living with Preschoolers*, and *Glacier Valley*. Mary works from her home in Polson, Montana, where she lives with her husband, Dan, who is a high school biology teacher, and their three children, Jennifer, Kevin, and Katie.

IT HAPPENED IN . . .

In a lively, easy-to-read style that is entertaining as well as informative, Falcon has separated the historical wheat from the chaff and served up highlights from the past.

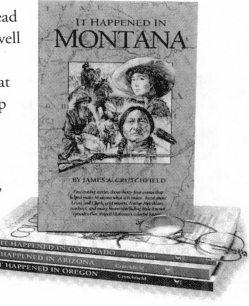

With six books in print, and more on the way, this series will give you insight into historical events that happened in your state. All books are written by author James A. Crutchfield.

IT HAPPENED IN ARIZONA	$8.95
IT HAPPENED IN COLORADO	$7.95
IT HAPPENED IN MONTANA	$7.95
IT HAPPENED IN NEW MEXICO	$8.95
IT HAPPENED IN OREGON	$8.95
IT HAPPENED IN WASHINGTON	$8.95